GOOD HARBOR

Max Heinegg

LILY POETRY REVIEW BOOKS

The Paul Nemser Prize is named for a master of the lyric narrative. Paul Nemser's most recent collection is *A Thousand Curves* from Red Mountain Press, spring 2021. His book *Taurus*, which won the New American Poetry Prize, was published by New American Press in 2013. His chapbook of prose poems, *Tales of the Tetragrammaton*, was published by Mayapple Press in 2014. Nemser's poems have appeared widely in magazines such as *AGNI*, *Blackbird*, *Linebreak*, *Poetry*, and *TriQuarterly*. We encourage you to seek out and read his work.

The Judge's Comments

Max Heinegg's *Good Harbor* is one of those rare collections of poems in which a confidence emerges almost immediately that we are in the hands of a poet who creates the sensation that life is writing itself. In a stance that manages to be at once wry and quizzical, tenderhearted and tough, the poet/speaker surveys, interrogates, analyzes, embraces, and recapitulates the torrid and balmy experience of the heart with poignancy and panache. The poems present with an intelligence that seeps ineluctably into one's ken— Heinegg's sagacity brews itself with a gentle muscularity and arises like steam from the cup. But the wisdom is not the totality of it—the poems also manifest a rip-roaring engagement with perception at the level of the five senses. How deeply gratifying it is to read these poems, an entire story (for really, all the poems here are episodes in the tale of a life) that does not end happily ever after, but finds its ends through the means of joy.

—Tom Daley, author of *House You Cannot Reach* and judge for the
  inaugural Paul Nemser Book Prize

For Wendy, Ava, and Stella

Table of Contents

I

II

An Hour is a Sea
Between a few, and me—
With them would Harbor be—

Emily Dickinson

I

The Spider of Damocles

You've been reading *The Year of Magical Thinking*
& tell me you want to die before the children,
& I agree. The one dread I'd ghost for, folding
my hand before dark who bluffs facetiously
but holds all. The riches of living simultaneously
is a luck worth more than any gravitas. I thought
how I'd end it if my trinity vanished & was ready
to ask if you'd Woolf it, or stammer out the days,
when above my head in a web the sunlight hid,
a three-inch spider between pole & sky said
eight *Easy tigers* to my tempting. Not a sword
above a laden table, not a tale the royals spun
to scare a vying naif, but the breath I shouldn't
second-guess. All happiness endangers itself.

Reverence

We keep no garden while the drought hammers
the yard to cinders. By day, rabbits stand
brazen in the clover, which means they number.
Here's where we dug deep to uproot the invasive
Norway maple, where we spliced raspberry bushes
the spiders now own, where we planted a fig tree
to learn we don't like figs, where the firewood
that has seen winter is seasoned into burning,
& where a diligence of insects colonizes
beneath the wood's brown tarp. What ends up
in the amber of our errors is the living
done. From the steps, I see where
the ice dams grew & poisoned the joist,
where the water sank down the railing & expanded,
but the cracked granite steps are our altar,
& these devotions are daily. We need no priest
to find the psalms or bend faith to reach us.
We are already singing the song we want to hear.

Remission

The cardinal is busy with what it can get,
& Father Christmas is on the computer shopping
for next year. I'm reading Campbell,
of the many & the one, no longer believing
every refraction is falsehood.
All religions are true, but none are literal.

By morning, we celebrate Sol Invictus
without knowing, our girls & the cousins wandering
the woods behind the house, the branches parting
an interpreted ceremony, breath catching itself at
the beauty in the wind. What is luck but
the light we've managed to be in the way of?

Inside, our daughter is off crushing *Twilight,*
& you're singing Albert Finney's *Scrooge,*
It isn't every day, good fortune comes my way
as your mother's cancer wig is passed around,
& the good society does not accept returns.
What hooks will be suspended in the coming year?

Our narrative is dedicated to what we escape.
She hints, *There is holly in the yard, if you want
to go & get it.* I do want to bring her the crown,
to see the berries less as blood, & to feel that
what we receive is worth what the world takes
away. I gather what I can & wreathe the green.

Ava at Eleven

The *puffy*, as the coat is called,
encases her in a navy-blue chrysalis,
her changes kept to herself.
Her arms balloon, pillowing her sleep.
The jacket's loose feathers, snow-stained
blue, were mine once. She's eleven
& will wear it to breakfast,
getting butter on the cuffs.

This morning, Ava wears the straight braid
you gave her, as directed.
Her ship rope of hair with auburn,
copper in its brown.
She walks herself to the bus stop.

Something lovely sleeps inside the gold
she surrounds herself with.
All year, we see little movement
in the orb about her, keeping
in her room, blankets draped from the top
bunk to the lower. These days
I knock. Until with luck,
she will claw her way out &
rest on us, letting her wings harden.

The Gauze Bow

Hair-tie in hand, she asks me to braid
because her IV arm won't bend.
By the door the nurses entered masked,

I part & clasp her curls, strawberry
blonde edged by lemons. She's surprised,
You did a pretty good job, Dad, but her bangs

fall in her eyes. I find the gauze bandage
her arm was wrapped in for the ride, &
improvise a simple bow from the roll.

Her pulse has climbed ahead of her
all day. I've followed every step, fearing
the virus or her body's response: the fever

cycles, the rash across her face. When
her scroll bores, she chooses the live-action
Cinderella, incognito in gifted clothes,

stunning the ball in iridescent blue. All night,
through the gaps in her red-flecked veil,
the fever breathes through. By morning,

her pulse calms. As she dreams of leaving,
the nurse asks her name, reading the blood aloud
to a girl unused to her gown.

Lockdown

For Joe Bowen, custodian

I tell the kids *stay calm* & lock the door,
find the red card to hang in the window
if need be & check for a path
to a gunless room—then direct them
to the corner by the bookshelf.

They sit on their hands, some girls on each other's laps,
spines close, all arms & shins—boys,
nearer to beauty than some will ever be
again. One will ask for music, one will ask to text
their mother, one will without asking. One will want
to & not. Together, close as empty desks. Kids
who trust that although I haven't learned all their names
yet, I would block the door for them.

Triptych After Golding

1.
In the public high school diaspora
the Sarahs walk, Egyptian, Haitian, Brazilian;
their mother tongues still sing in their middle names:
Esmael, Nehemie, Pinheiro.

My latest Sarah is tired from Ramadan,
says she can't wait for Eid al-Fitr
& hands me her *Lord of the Flies* mask project,
its symbols chosen to expose our dual nature,
ink flowers pushed through light to stand
for the shadows she encounters on the streets
to get to unmonitored hallways.

She knows I love her work, flourishes
to the edge of the cardboard. Her mask is more
assertion of who she already is. In her hijab,
she's curtained from her peers, focused on their own
awkward, emergent flesh, thinking only of
how they are perceived.

2.
On a good day, being the lone adult
on the island is Edenic. I'm asked at parties
how I *handle them.* Is high school still like
Lord of the Flies? Are there Rogers
in the hallways, stuffing freshmen into lockers?
Brass knuckles & weed, coerced blowjobs &
bullying? Thin slicing at *our* kids
who gather on Winthrop, brown by the bus,
assuming from their daps they are separate tribes,
everyone there although none want to be:
the Irish, Italians, Black, Brazilians, (the town's braid),
& the new strands: Tibetans, Syrians, Vietnamese, Indian—

Rohin who survived cancer of the septum,
Ellis, Jeremiah, & Taraji, who rap.
Maybe this is, as my old boss mocked,
the great American high school.

3.
If *nomen est omen,* any adult sees it coming—
all the shadows gathering
for a boy who's never named.

Marked, he still braves it,
from the smashed camp to Castle Rock,
to speak his peace against *the silvery laughter.*
Above the sea, he stands
defenseless *in the great hand of God,*
who lets the beast inspire obedient boys
to step on the lever.

When the boulder strikes,
my classes cleave.

For me, it falls for eleven chapters &
is still falling.

Ms.

They say they fire up joints in the back row,
that on the first floor you can hear the books
fall from her window where they're casting
ballots against the teachers' union.

They say she reads the *Oedipus* cycle
aloud, that one by one the heads drop
to the desk like leaves, after *Colonus*,
her analysis is the *coup de grace*.

They say she taught the grandparents,
the parents, & now they funnel
her the stragglers, lowering the last
hurdle to let them finish the race.

They say her charges turn a pass for water
into a jaunt down the halls of C building,
that you can hear them rattle the lockers
sounding lost as they call after girls.

Yet everyone wants to know if she's still there.
When they hear she is, not a syllable sinister,
& last year, when she fell on her way in,
the children shuddered for her bones.

She was back the next day, pulling her cart
of books & papers, to her room in this castle
on the hill that they say was built by a man
who perfected prisons in California.

Dreamer

For _____

She doesn't want to write "the Immigration essay,"
says she can't remember Governador Valadares.
She attended the local elementary, only learning
what she was when she couldn't work. Then it made sense,
her father praying when a cop followed his pickup,
her mother cleaning because she could without a card.

She wants to write about DACA, Trump stealing
her dream of staying, going to Berklee, becoming
a musician & then, a teacher. *Like you did.*
I'm afraid she should hide her history, leave
no paper trail. Now my help endangers her.

She decides to redact nothing, not because I've taught her
God is in the details, but because she knows
there is nothing illegal about her. At home,
my daughters walk from their bus together.
There are raids one town over. I want them to know
what the country is becoming, what it's not worth.

Keepers of the House

The day the keepers of the house tremble and those that look out of windows
be darkened, because man goeth to his long home, and the mourners go about
the streets —Ecclesiastes 12:5

In his apron, Vincent plucks the vivid Italian cookies,
doubting correctly *They're for my girls,*
& slaps his gut, *Nothing wrong with a sweet tooth.*
His name's tattooed elbow to wrist in cursive,
neck adorned by a thin gold
cross, telling me *the drugs* are why he left town.
Turning into Gloucester…poison just handed out to kids.

I hear you. I've read the epitaphs of morning texts,
learned the limits of a teacher's influence,
& haven't seen the last of the young shadows
like the one my colleague follows
home from school, trailing the specter
of powder & the silence of a son,
like the two ghosts in my classroom who return

to take their seats when I open the window
for the breeze. When they're listening, I preach:
trust yourself, speak, don't court danger,
but I'm talking to myself. I regret I never told them
that I used to relish that back-tongue bitterness,
taking emptiness for oasis. Friends died,
but I was lucky. When I needed safety, I still had keys

to the house I couldn't wait to leave.

The Electric Heart

Typical of me to not know the heart
is electric, thinking wires & Edison,
halogens & stadiums were the only
dizzying grids. One step toward black-out
& quickly back from grief, your father's luck
to faint & crack his skull on a doorstep,
one turn from his own. So, the thread rebounds,
the scissor slips, unsteady, blood dizzied
in winter snow & he will be fitted
with a defibrillator to shock his heart
back, should its current fail. We visit him
at Ellis, & walk a hall of wires & white
walls, every outlet filled, more machines
than patients. Kind nurses keep their rounds,
appear on muted soles, soften static.
His surgery is planned, but may be moved,
the days in O.R. are hard to predict,
she notes. He's spry, quick-witted, ordering
roast beef on one elbow, talking about
next week's lighter schedule; work nonetheless.

Outside the window, gray birds & their young
use the thin stone ledge to wait out the rain.

Winter Reeds

From the driver's side, the night's legato
until a field of stumps where corn stalks rose
staccato the quarter mile. Then *phragmites
australis* abut—long reeds loose between
marsh teeth play the wind as it is written:
a hollow chorus of once & again
perennials, roadside grasses swaying
in the season. How many have we left
to drive between our parents' Christmases,
happy enough to feel safe complaining?
Near the end of the plot, a sudden mist rises
from the rushes where only darkness was,
night sounds in the car we can't place, a window
a child left open, the wind across the wood.

The Ground is Never Too Cold to Dig

1.
It's been seventeen years. A memory
is not what you remember, just the last
time you remember it. The ground
only seems frozen, the cold
only seems strong.

2.
In my grandfather's chair by the fireplace,
my father told me the machines can smash
frozen ground, that the gravediggers
didn't want to work to break the earth;
the ground is never too cold to dig.

3.
Later, the city intervened, so we dressed,
made our way to the grave where
the uncle we never saw lost his speech
& had to extemporize.
It went badly; we sympathized,

when words cannot feed
the starved moment. We buried
my grandfather beside his wife of fifty years,
while his second wife stood beside us.
I never saw her again.

4.
The service ended & a light snow settled.
Amid the wine at 15 Second Street,
the priest, who played Santa Claus
each Christmas, told my wife
she had beautiful brown eyes.

Ferberizing

Ten steps from my howling daughter,
I wait it out, as I have been
expressly told to.

The first drink of the evening is poured
& will stay untouched unless this works.

The sky considers twilight & goes there
inexorably.
Children consider sleep & go there,
perhaps.

So, I listen outside the door
for the turning of your breath
that crests into a small suffering
I could end, but I let you
teach yourself to fall into peace,
to accept at this moment
less than the desired.

I know the other side of tears
is a valley where shields of trees
wield shade for you.

So, may you sleep there.

Night Fishing

I look, you look, he looks; we look, ye look, they look.
                                                —Melville, *Moby Dick*

We'll know in ten minutes if the false moon
we submerge from the dock's edge in Pigeon Cove
will draw them in to hunt the way moonlight does,
& has through the ages, stars & moon sinking
through the waters' boundary to refract & mint
these night hunters the coins of their eyes.
If not, we'll depart Rockport for Magnolia,
but a fleet storms the dock, translucent darts
two fingers long, single fins for crowns.

Each sees the squid in his own way, Ahab's
doubloon pinned to the mast *as a medal of the sun.*
Micah sees a feast but first distributes poles,
& orchestrates lines for his unseasoned crew.
Everett, seven, is after the Kraken but drags the blue
net's webbing across the top of the water.

Ava sees it as a fearful loveliness, tiny ghosts
lifted from a darkness that inks her mother's dress.
Stella sees avoidance, furious at the squid
for not biting, she reels around the dock, jostling
Freddie sees it as a conjuring but believes
in being in the prime position.
When Stella admits defeat, she does not sulk,
but takes the squid's milky mantle from the hooks
for others, pinching the boy cousins' jobs.

Over the blackening bucket the unhooking
is not grisly, the motion a swivel.
Calvin sees his skill as a mark of progress,
frees my four squid fluidly, & calls out *Sup bruh,*
to his uncle sipping lager, who returns the salute.

I sidle up to Wendy but she's after a catch.
I know as she courses, she plays a dark game
imagining a dorsal fin taking the water's pulse.

Fisher, four, sees it with his father's ease
& unhooks his own, & Phoebe, six, surveying
on the edge of the dock sees dozens careen
by like a bird that at any moment could choose one

fortune in this age to find the otherworldly
so close, where once we cast sights on the leviathan,
a brave voyage away. Now, at our fingers
the murky world unites beast & man, grappling
on the hooks we sink beneath the luminous
screen that reveals no frozen spaces, squid
bursting like synapses, finning like neurons,
swimming the vicious infinite in microcosm.

Above us, the Big Dipper's clarion,
& the pale school lingers on the trailing shadows.
Our bucket's half full, but it's past the hour
the youngest fray, so one last cast,
not for the squid Melville's Dagoo saw
monstrous on the surface, nor for the giant
that clamped down on Nemo's Nautilus,

but for another glimpse of this spectral navy,
passing silver through a cove near the ocean
where the great chain has fallen
& centuries slip between intricate links,
separation razed, great distances folded
for local boats held fast by small anchor.

& I'd stay by that pale gathering to catch another,
not for greed or even the peace of fishing,
but for the reason I turn from my bed
to awaken my phone at night, to send my hook down
for another message, to test my line to see
if there's another tug, to pose another living
question surfacing to a captured insight
or newly beheld fear I recognize by the light
of where I stand, or stood,
to set the dark in motion, & stare,
transfixed, the ocean come to me.

Sanibel

Cajole me in from the porch of shore
to tiptoe over daggering shells,

following the sun's andante
into the pickling. From waves

to troughs, I enter the measure
to keep up with the conductor,

calling rest an accord. Out of doubt's
earshot, I don't wonder, *Did we leave*

too few lovers? Any other one too many.
Young, we left together. Now our verses

double as chorus—the song carries itself.
At night, we follow our daughters

down the beach beneath a parting
moon, the darkness all our palace.

At Last, I Discover My Parents Are Ancient Egyptians

I finally see what they were working at,
the stories about being raised by nuns,
my father's lost seven years as a Jesuit,
lightly whipping himself before bed—
the mortification of the flesh,
& then his vitriol for Abraham.

The signs were everywhere. They staggered
the house with surprising wine—who drinks
Vouvray? & stacked the attic
with Iranian rugs, the photo from Tehran
where my mother was pelted
for walking with bare arms.

Their rooms were full of the symbols
& ornaments of myth—the African statues,
their court of cats, named deceptively:
Horatio, Achilles, Daisy.
But when they dubbed the petite
lioness Sekhmet, "she who mauls,"

the jig was up. Now I see the empty
hand-blown glass vases as canopic,
the eternal pantry bursting with basil
pesto, olive oils, dried creminis,
champagne vinegars & two-pound honey
jars to wait in amber patience

among odd provisions for the feast to come.
In her costume jewelry are the amulets,
& in his tomes the Book of the Dead—
somewhere in the rows of Russian, Yiddish,
German, the book that might contain
the answers should the soul forget

when they walk into the Hall of Two Truths
to speak with the Eater of Shadows,
the Breaker of Stones, & list the offenses
they did not give: *I did not feign enthusiasm;*
I did not hold my tongue; I did not fear solace;
I did not stop singing; I did not beat

the children; I did not abandon the other.
When, after the feather is judged
no heavier than their hearts, may their priests
unwrap them & let them walk through
the gates & into the delta, past the wet rushes,
into the effortless field of reeds.

Her Airport Will

Every time she plans their flight,
my mother unearths their long-known will
& emails it to me. I don't think about death
& flying, I trust, happier in their 70s
that she's still booking, but it's too much
gravity to read my father's choice
of funeral music: Brandenburg,
beside my mother's mode of burial: cremation.

I prefer her airport will, which she composes
at the gate, each time I take
their wheeled luggage out of the trunk
& send them off—a flurry of
clarifications: who gets her jewelry,
the Indian rings, the costume pieces
& *the good stuff*; how the women
(my wife, sister, & daughters) are to play
Solomon & divide Persian rugs,
my grandfather's ring, the ancient dog,
the untuned piano, the religious icons
that no one in the house worships,
the Corn god, Centeotl, two cats
& the porcelain bathtub
they just don't put in houses nowadays.

How her expectation is that a man
will take care of himself. How the concern
over one's dead parents would be material first—
as if we'll be remembered by what we leave,
when that is what will be forgotten.

Cliff Jumping

I want risk until I arrive, my bad
vantage doubled.
Add six feet of frame to the fall,
& now we're talking. Eye's measure
no marker, but courage is
not listening to the bluster
of air, not gauging
the arbitrary leap & pussyfoot
on the mossy stone—
edge as much as I dislike, what the group will
decide
is the criterion. My daughter flying
into the lake's silver
registers what I do with my fear.
Thought is a leaning that gets me
no closer.
The distance twitches.

II

Wyf Thinks of Summer

She spells it the old way, calls our girl a Viking
warrior, proclaims our halls safe, restores the day's
initial mystery, calls the sunny two-bed Mexico,
paints *All sorrow is less with bread* in our kitchen,
makes a den of the ten-month year, & bravely
brings them forth. She won't lie & say she doesn't
bask in the exhaust of the last bus, but once
vacation starts, it's slippery. Then August ads drop
the taunt of where we're all headed, friends
secretly pleased our lease's up & it's the grind
'til holidays give the pause no one challenges.
In December, when the chimney draws, she tends
the light down to the word's coals, plays Hestia
& paces the interim of our state's cold spring,
but when June alights on the North Shore tides,
she wakes to chart them as they rise, inclines to
hear the salt-water music, not yet beginning to end.

Cassiopeia

Over a dock in Islamorada, winter shows us
the Hunter's badge of stars,
his shield & cudgel raised, but not needed
against the mortal Scorpius, whose tail
sleeps in summer skies. Tonight,

I remember Orion's other death,
the target when Apollo taunted
a smitten sister, *Bet you can't*
pierce that dot in the distance which
was her lover's head above water,
as he swam in peace, miles away.
Her immortal grief couldn't sway Zeus
to bring him back, but in honor,
her father strung the stars.

On the steps back, we pause to catch
the circumpolar queen mother,
who only boasted once that her girl
outclassed the holy spirits of the sea,
rousing their father to revenge.
Young, I thought that myth only
how wealth makes one feel untouchable.

The night sky should be the end of hubris
& the jealous possession that rules us,
but this is one of the last times
their inseparable youth & beauty are ours entirely,
before they quit their rooms & cleave to others.
Now I know silence is a safer vanity, & why
she had forgotten what the world is
ready to take away. Yet,
a ruinous secret, I too
love my daughters more than I fear the gods.

Garlic

I bury it face up
before the spring frost, so
each clove becomes a head,
as in Cadmus, where each seeded
dragon tooth erupts a warrior.

We clip & fry the scapes but also wait
to pull the hard-necks & dry them
in the shed. Sharpening
as divided, or coddled
in foil, gold pulp for our bread,

but charred in oil-smoke, an insult—
lingering
lily of the pyramids,
fifteen pounds for a slave,
scorodon to the Greeks,

poultice to a centurion,
or chewed to whet a killing
lust, & afterwards, felt
a sifting in the blood. *Allium*,
those legions called for it

after salting the fields, planting
courage in the doomed Celts.
Then Alaric found the Roman gates
& the long ships went both ways
on the whale-road, as the old Germans sang.

So, the Angles named the island England
& the sea-axe named its tribe—
their double-tongue mothers mine,
whose war-eyes saw the *spear-leek*
a weapon in the ground.

Sous

I peel, you dice.
After a quarter century
here, I am in charge when she asks me
because *someone who has eaten may still be hungry.*

She calls me over to test if the carrot's sweet,
to try *her Czech* tomatoes that Peter dug.

We work & don't
discuss the doctors, who I distrust
based on geography, thinking Boston might save her
years that Upstate won't.

There was a time when the novelty of a man
in the kitchen wore off, & she'd leave
the room as I left it, the mess my own rejoinder.
But when I picked up on it, she showed me
vinegar is added to hot potatoes,
that broccoli salad needs sugar.

I still skip the deep prep, don't start
Thanksgiving the week of. I know the roots
are salted mid-saute, & mind how much
distraction tastes—so I should remember
to adjust, as she does, keeping a cloth
on the counter, tasting as I go.

Saw

A hammer whose head flies
off, but the handle is genuine
hickory, a gift that survived

your father who oils the antique,
treats the broken as gently
used. His vintage, edgeless

skis for Steve to telemark
an unwaxed fourteen
miles into Marcy Dam.

For Becky, the cloth-top LeBaron
convertible, dubbed The Kevorkian,
to spin Vermont winters

in two-wheel drive, & this orange
shed denizen he sees wasted,
steel only sleeping in

thin covers of rust, still
dreaming of branches. Incisors
loose as milk teeth,

it would choke on anything but
kindling. He tells us it sang
in the splinters. *Perfectly good* saw.

Window Guests

1.
Near summer, we allowed the sparrows
my wife called, affectionately, *dirt birds*
to nest behind our second floor AC—
we woke at five to their conference.

My neighbor asked if I thought it wise,
& more loath to offend than to disturb,
I unscrewed the plastic accordion edge
& floated the light braids of twig & leaf
to the herb garden, but after, I found
a powdery blue egg on the nursery ledge,
& having overstepped, left it there.

That evening, we drove our brood to range
beneath the strawberry moon
the Algonquin named for the berries' peak,
& the only one we'll see for seventy years.
Unimpressed, the girls scampered down
Robbins Farm Park's hill as we picked it,
admiring *pink pink pink.*

2.
Teachers on the hill in June & Boston marked
the moon in its clear field, the talk of last bells,
summer schemes & students floating away,
classroom windows clear again.

On the longest night of the year
the science teacher found Mars, Jupiter, & Saturn
with ease, its rings to her a single gold star.
A bad student myself, I feigned facility, turning
back to the straw beneath the berry.
She told me that since I'd touched the egg,
the parents would never warm to it again.

In July, the dirt birds returned, their stark
alarm set for dawn. We let them stay.

Bedroom View

I'd be above it all but for the wires
her easement grants to halve our share of sky
to keep hers clear. When I called in the Grid,
they wanted a ransom for our own poles—
she dubbed it Wiregate, how I minded
hers, an eyelash I could keep across my eye.

Otherwise, she's kindness, rarely home,
her better grill's unfired. From our second story,
I follow how the fulcrum also coaxes cedar
waxwings to rest outside the circumscribed
space. Remember how we privileged openness
& uprooted the maple, called it invasive?

Revenged, it willed us her electric.
Did a tipped worker string the branches? Perhaps
they knew, but as it was so high, let
aged gazes fall. My eyes also
dowse, down to earth to divine
from the trampled yard, memory's source

where brief gardens pulsed & summer knit
us three sheets by the fire-pit, where kindergarten
nudes stung Catholic parents. Out of love
with its audience, it now resembles us:
not above imposition, beneath
lawful wires our minds trick invisible.

Lake George

The season's drive through Vermont,
then to Woodstock for sandwiches, past the gazers
at Quechee Gorge, no stopping for Scottish sweaters
or thirty-dollar handles of maple syrup.
Off the exit, past the Stewart's, Whitehall's rotting
houses crouch on broken joists, house fronts double
as storefronts, bicycles lean without chains.
This is also New York.

Next Putnam & the hills, the long climb
past the pig farm & its insult of methane
that makes Stella laugh, the two-mile descent
past farms in doubtful states of operation,
curling along Lake Road to Link Way,
the house bought with cash found stashed
in a basement pipe, left by Peter's father,
Irving, who worked at GE & mistrusted banks
& died of a heart attack from union strife.
Vivian found the pipe & bought the plot.
The camp was built by hand.

In a boat driven by my ten-year old
with her grandpa's help, the mind a rudder
as we move through the medium of water,
the background of what we call the shining path,
not *sendero luminoso*, but seven o'clock
lightness in light, smashed into sequins
by dock jumpers & Sable, the aging black lab.

Stand distanced from the working life
& if not for light, come for summer's
single-mindedness, the insistent song of heat,
to build a beehive pizza oven out of mud
with Uncle Micah; to assist children who cast

for sunfish until the hooking; to run
to Smith camp & gaze on the untended
grape vines, to lay stone steps with Peter
& Carolyn & Wendy, rolling small boulders
up the walk, raising a bottle to Sisyphus.

Years past, when the camp was empty,
we'd wake to see the black waters crossing
the bay without us, & composed ourselves
on its surface. In time, we took your grand-
mother's bedroom, our children in the bunk
beside, assured her ghost kept us company.
Once, I thought of family as a tree from whose
heights we fell, but now we are the tree itself.
Our roots seek water, sourcing the known ground.

Easter Afternoon

When my wife slid the daunting needle into her childless
sister's side, we kept our ease quiet. Now their trinity
ranges loud across the yard, & it's a blessed stretch

to walk their youngest toward the egg, barely hidden
gold at the feet of Jesus, the two-foot concrete statue
they found facedown, lifted, & treat as auspicious.

Even if there was no hunt, faith would take finding
behind the wetland, more of a swamp beside
a coop the foxes emptied, one layer at a time.

Now I stand by the Son in the same bodhisattva pose,
heart pinned to his robe, the cross's victorious
standard, but his arm is broken off in the pine needles.

I'd return his open hand, but I'm holding the cherub's,
& carrying her plastic basket's haul, forgotten when
she targets a miniature castle & an immediate siege

succeeds, the sweetest clutch. In unseasonable heat,
the garden's fake owl scares fruit-thieves from theirs,
but North Shore tomatoes now grow until November.

Denial's as ubiquitous as rebirth, the grass a deep green
overnight. For us, long summers & longer falls, but when
we've shaded the earth, who will move the boulder? After

Good Harbor, the boy cuts us cucumbers with a butter knife,
& my better's lovely, bare-kneed in April, musing whose birth
is fairest. *Any, safely delivered.* My brother-in-law tells me, when

his is caught in brambles, how the Germans joyed at dawn but
still set the children's gems in nettles. She plucks them off,
so eager each capture feels the first, no tears at the sight of thorns.

The Lifeguards of Gull Bay

The lifeguards of Gull Bay preserve their rule
of indolence. Perhaps sixteen, they're
the only children left on the beach
scarfing Sun Chips, Lean Cuisine, & Cokes
but flat-stomached, kicking the sandcastles
our children leave. They rake false waves
into Sandy Beach & remind parents off
for a walk, there is no leaving twelve-year-olds
alone—demanding six-year-olds remove kayaks,
keeping a folder in the chair for grievances,
filing away summer visitors as effete.

It's true: my brother-in-law's stowed gin,
the history teacher is building The Great Wall,
but before us is Blythewood— the compound
rumored sold to Kate Hudson, vacant—so
no Craftsmans anchor, no Black Crowes dock,
no spying Goldie Hawn on the widow's walk
from which the bay is clear. We're teachers
on dry land run by teenagers, muttering about
ideal summer. Only, when they're gone,
we send our kids back to kick up the waves.

Fireworks

Tonight, on the 4th, the wealthier Hague
gifts a glittering largesse to Lake George,
& sings *the sky is falling* to our children
reassuringly. We watch from the boat,
how the spires are upturned jars of color,
dripping into upside-down umbrellas.

This spark, teasing the eyes,
came to us by caravan down the skeins
of the Silk Road, from Northwest China
where first they boomed bamboo shoots
in fire to frighten ghosts, then alchemists,
mixing a potion for immortality

blended saltpeter, sulfur, & charcoal into
rockets for the Mongols. Then on to Western
Persia, to the Crusades, blasted Christians
in the 11th century. Later, Europe coronated
in the blooms, while cannons mastered butchery.
Our children will not accept the ending,

Is this the finale? No, this! The chandeliers,
ghostly, gone; the last smoke trails after
lingering holiday drunks ash out & so what began
as spectacle ends in darkness. Carolyn's left
us a floodlight, so our boat will find the bay—
joy consumed, talk still turning to embers.

Good Harbor

Sandbar to sandbar on the last day of August
we walk Good Harbor—
then, resting, elbows in sand
at noon, the smell of Gloucester: salty
ocean, cigarettes, & tanning oil.

We work to scatter brazen gulls
that snatch a sandwich from an adult's hand.
Small boys steer kites into the sand.

Wendy gets a text that our niece Phoebe
is in the ER. She's eaten lily of the valley berries,
which we did not know are poisonous;
they slow the heart, cause hallucinations,
& line our rocky backyard, beside belladonna,
the danger we recognize. Becky writes,
I never even saw it in her hands.

The waves rock & collapse
with the weight of our worry, but we hide this
from the kids, take a beach walk to the bridge
where older couples walk, comfortably
shirtless with paunches. Eventually all of us
see that shame is pointless & self-inflicted.

Returning, we join the line for lemon ices,
tip the college student, eye the tide.

Becky texts that Phoebe is safe now.
My daughter's tooth rocks in her mouth,
loose enough to see the hinge.

On a beach swarming with people,
a child holding an orange pail calls out
to her mother, *I don't want to be alone!*

Naturally

They assuredly well-become the land they inhabit.
　　—Charles Darwin, on the marine iguanas of the Galapagos

I twitch into the couch as the hawk descends &
talons through the iguana's body, repurposed
for the peckish, tongues out for the blood.
He's only doing it for his babies, mine explains.

We learn the iguanas landed on the archipelago
by hanging onto driftwood—blown across the ocean,
now they hold their breath for minutes, gnawing blue
algae off underwater rocks, chewing water-mouthed.

Some get rocked unconscious by dickhead seals, some drown,
but most find the ebb, sinking adapted claws in
crevices, & scale their way up to bask, victors
on basalt, sneezing rockets out the excess salt.

By night, they sleep, body to body, in burrows.
After an age away from home, we four sleep
in a mess of legs, writhe out from bed-sweat
to take the light's commands. Soon, they'll grasp

the way their mother & I fell, into the open,
our skin's dignity to dive & return, stealing heat
in our salty wigs, these whitening crowns,
in the dorsal scales of our starched clothes.

A Stranding

Rare for Gloucester, we found the common dolphin's
frozen body beside a lost child's hat, fifty feet up
from Lighthouse Beach of Annisquam, the *top of the rock*

where to the left *vineland* emerges—Wingaersheek,
whose name is bird & body in the shoreline, cold
trembling for you. His black tongue juts,

hardened to indignance, the smile only an underbite,
gray hourglass flanks a gift only a vulture can open,
the crows & gulls content with eyes. *How did he end up here?*

Chasing fish in the wading pools? Stranded on the ebb
until he lay beside the Irish moss in the driftwood's brush?
Below him, we see the small holes in the sand from birds'

beaks, the wider ones breathing clams my nephew crushes
with his sister's yellow toy shovel. The side of the good
mammal peels, only the season stays his disintegration.

Did he miss a flood that would have returned him
with its rising, or did hunger tell an irresistible lie:
that he had enough time before the falling tide?

Joy Division

The body above the graves
of Oak Grove Cemetery
holds its post. No hangdog
face, no fretful ghost
in the light. It does not shine
a reminder. A biding,
If not today, perhaps tomorrow.

My daughter lowers her mask & says,
It's peaceful here, & shows me
a rose quartz headstone,
private by the pines.

Distancing this spring, she discovered
the older plots & family vaults
blocks from our house. I thought
too dark, her walks listening to *Love
Will Tear Us Apart,* but that's the draw
for both of us, melody stained
away from brightness.

I know these dead saw worse
omens come true. Wars we choose
to know about. Soldiers too soon
shorn threads. This daylight
moon says some curses are just
the worm turning the soil
for a crop we'll never see.

That's fair, her phrase returns
to me. This isn't a plague, &
I don't believe in curses. The moon
keeps our quiet, looking on like
a father, but only a follower.

Dogtown

Were the trees always this macabre,
the witch wrists of beech & pine
stands so ragged when the widows &
their faithful named the windings down
past the reservoir & the moraines?
Babson's Finnish masons left us 1930s
inculcation that no longer cuts it.

COURAGE is hidden in the woods.
INDUSTRY is a more level stone
than *SPIRITUAL POWER,* but notice
their closeness. *INTELLIGENCE* is to
not take a selfie by it, but Fisher says it's fine
at the top. My daughter sits on *IDEAS,*
my winsome niece on *STUDY,* mom's favorite.

BEON TIME allows no spaces.
My first thought's Beyonce, then Beorn,
then beyond. Dogtown, once dubbed
for the company the animals gave
while the men warred, winds on past
where we're willing to go. So follow
the way back across the railroad, & walk

between the rails, ponds on each side, no cars
in the distance. A lab is posed by *LOYALTY,*
& it's pleased to be pleasing. The platitudes don't
account for birth. Luck is talk of a shelter pup,
not having to break promises to a child.

The Sunday path the rich planned to inspire
virtue is nowhere without a map.

Clouds

I play them the live version, comparing 1969
to today. They believe in the advertised mantle,
the powwow of stars. As the cycle goes, weather.
What do they think of Joni's manner, confidence
in her own tuning, how she starts with the familiar
clouds, then *illusions,* & then *love?* Much of adulthood
is looking at the last lines first, dowsing the cracked
ground for strategy. They doze the talk from a desk's
divan, don't marvel at her ascent to cirrus, the surety
of one above, who falls how she wants to, in liquid
grace notes through the weight-bearing gray. How
my mind stays the beautiful song & its singer
ageless. The challenge when my yearlings
wonder at the gifted water, debating thirst.

Vernon's Quarry

There's a *Steal Your Face* on the boulder
above the blue-black water
to tell us this place is for *heads,*
or teens up from Plum Cove
away from their fathers, sinking
beneath Gloucester's powdery stars.

Tonight, we hear what they smoke
to amplify, hit music beneath
an ignorance of rock. Some dive headfirst
but that's a gamble, the bottom's sooner
than seen. I know age has made me
jealous. House-sitting, kids asleep

in the next room while I pace the edge myself,
sensing my weight on the waveless surface
of rest—the inheritance I've spent
one night at a time. Tomorrow
will return, a wastrel still
in love with his travels like a cloud.

Higher Ground

For J.A.

In high school, we'd smoke & sink into his moon chairs.
We'd learned the word *ennui*, & would declare joy-
eyed & canine, *Ennui, I am stoned.*

At a Kinderhook party, in a farmer's field
we choked down mushroom tea
& doffed our clothes to stand in mud
petting a cow that became a bull,
& retraced our steps to dress & trample in
to Maia's, her father playing *Blood on the Tracks.*

We dropped acid in Portland & I made my peace
offering, jamming on his Stratocasters to "Fire
On the Mountain." I hated The Dead,
but I stuck to the rhythm, so he could descend
the frets in Jerry's mixolydian. A decade passed.

He would message, threaten to visit
on his motorcycle, asking why buying drugs
had to involve violence. *Couldn't people just sell it
& be cool?* In my thirties, sedate on legal ones,
I kept him at a distance, answering his emails late
while looking at my flowering yard. A twinge
when he arrived, glazed
over in Somerville, in cop sunglasses.

He showed me his time in Thailand, underwater
films, training Navy SEALs to scuba-dive.
His otherworldly life, his haywire mind,
his second wife who died in the tsunami,
while the animals, sensing it,
found higher ground.
Not up to me to intervene.

At the Glenville Queen, on antidepressants,
he was a dimly lit McMurphy. The waitress
asked if he was alright—our love fired indignant.

My mother said there was a photo of us
hugging by the service altar. I never saw that,
but there is the Central Park Rose Garden
prom shot I keep in my work desk,
in a tuxedo for one of the two times in my life.
We're laughing the way that always made me cough
& tear. He was a black belt, but even drunk,
would never show me how to fight.
When I'd ask him, he'd say, *Run away.*

Expectations

You ask me if I remember what to do
with your body when you die?
What if I go first?

You won't, & make me promise
to give your ashes to the waters you love:
one half for Lake George,
one half for Good Harbor,
the local remembrance, & then,
ocean, oblivion.

At dinner, when the retelling
of the day becomes drama, our daughters
ask, *Why does it always have to be oblivion?,*
the word an inside joke, how we're too
expressive, every problem operatic.

They're right though, we take *this shit
deadass.* Raised missing religion,
we chase the sacred because we are
the ones who'd ruin the commune
for not sticking to its founding
principles—vowing to the waves
to trade ashes for passage,
knowing our children will have to
help us reach the other.

The Apple Tree at Bar Harbor

Where the tide turns out its pockets,
this prosperous one stands,
roots upending stone, loaded branches
a stone's throw from smug
lawns that extend a tenancy built
against the ledge. Tourists speak French &
German. You talk to me about the way
the West will never be returned
to the single voice of experience,
nature & the mind of one being born,

but the body, having learned too early
its loneliness, stays merely Earth's
fearful admirer. Taught to be guarded,
man less than woman. Bedeviled together,
we wonder at the East, raised without sin,
who live seeing the fruit as a gift, just
a misty welcome on the stem, & eat
the sense's peace down to the seeds,
feeling no separation. In the fog, our girls
race the edge, tempted to shake the tree.

Blueberrying

Gorham Mountain, Acadia

Happy on the incline,
we sprawl—

bad goats
on the summit's side,
chewing each tiny burst
off-balance, our kids'
sneakers crushing white lichen.

We take no pictures, leave joy
unlocked
for others to discover
summer's pride
in the ephemeral.

While hikers above
talk of the good salt
air resting in panorama,
we offer each other
all we have in our hands.

Acknowledgments

"The Spider of Damocles"   *Free State Review*

"Reverence"   *Algebra of Owls*

"Birds & Boundaries"   *Sweet Tree Review*

"Dear V."   *Gravel*

"Remission"   *Borderlands*

"Ava at 11"   *Nine Mile Magazine*

"The Gauze Bow"   *Midwest Quarterly*

"Lockdown"   *American Journal of Poetry*

"Triptych After Golding"   *Nine Mile Magazine*

"Ms."   *The Lake (UK)*

"Dreamer"   *Cultural Weekly*

"Keepers of the House"   *Nixes Mate*

"The Electric Heart"   *Poetry Quarterly*

"Winter Reeds"   *Stone Canoe*

"The Ground is Never Too Cold to Dig"   *San Pedro River Review*

"Ferberizing"   *Sweet Tree Review*

"Night Fishing"   *The Cortland Review*

"Sanibel"   *Twyckenham Notes*

"At Last, I Discover My Parents
   Are Ancient Egyptians"   *Stone Canoe*

"Her Airport Will"   *Stone Canoe*

"Cliff Jumping"   *Fourth & Sycamore*

"Wyf Thinks of Summer"   *Nixes Mate*

"Cassiopeia"   *Sidney Lanier Poetry Award
   (First place)*

"Garlic"   *Nazim Hikmet Competition*

"Sous"   *Misfit Magazine*

"Saw"   *Sow's Ear Poetry Review*

"Window Guests"   *Pangyrus*

"Bedroom View"   *Ibbetson Street Press*

"Lake George"   *Fourth & Sycamore*

"Easter Afternoon"   *Nazim Hikmet Competition*

"The Lifeguards of Gull Bay"   *Muddy River Poetry Review*

"Fireworks"   *Louisiana Literature*

"Good Harbor"   *Main Street Rag*

"A Stranding"   *The Shore*

"Joy Division"
    (previously titled "Satellite")   *32 Poems*

"Dogtown"   *The Banyan Review*

"Clouds"   *The Maynard*

"Vernon's Quarry"   *Nine Mile Magazine*

"Higher Ground"   *Rougarou Journal*

"Expectations"   *Cultural Daily*

"The Apple Tree at Bar Harbor"   *Midwest Review*

"Blueberrying"   *Nimrod*

About the Author

Max Heinegg was born in Cooperstown, NY, and raised in Schenectady, NY. He received his BA from Union College in 1995 and his MAT from Boston University in 1998. He has been teaching middle and high school English in the Medford Public Schools since 1998.

His poems have been nominated for the Pushcart Prize and Best of the Net. He has won the Sidney Lanier Poetry Award, the Emily Stauffer Poetry Prize, and was a finalist for the poetry prizes of *Asheville Poetry Review, December Magazine, Crab Creek Review, Cultural Weekly, Rougarou Journal, Cutthroat Journal, Twyckenham Notes, West Virginia Writers,* and the Nazim Hikmet Prize.

He is also a singer-songwriter whose records can be heard at www.maxheinegg.com

He lives in Medford, MA with his wife and two daughters.

CPSIA information can be obtained
at www.ICGtesting.com
Printed in the USA
LVHW051738100322
713135LV00014B/1887